MW00626069

Choose Wisely
No Matter What The Odds Are:
The 1st 20 Years

By: Rahim Thompson

©2021 by Rahim Thompson
ALL RIGHTS RESERVED

All rights reserved. No part of this publication may be reproduced, distributed, or transmitted in any form or by any means, including photocopying, recording, or other electronic or mechanical methods, without the prior written permission of the publisher, except in the case of brief quotations embodied in critical reviews and certain other noncommercial uses permitted by copyright law. For permission requests, contact Rahim Thompson at R.thompson@thechosenleague.com

ISBN: 978-0-578-86145-6

Cover Illustrator:
        Zuliesuivie Ball

Editors:
        Zuliesuivie Ball
        Carolyn Ball
        Samuel Allen

Table of Contents

I was born deaf with a broken foot.

I have been homeless.

I have been ridiculed for my religious beliefs.

I have been laughed at for sharing my ambition and goals.

I have been hit by a truck.

I have cried.

I have doubted myself.

Through all of that, I have risen and, in the process, helped others and instilled belief and faith in those who doubted themselves.

Chapter 1: Hello World.

On August 29, 1976 I was born in Glen Cove Community Hospital in New York to Octavia Mary Danielson, a single parent of a 10-year-old girl, my sister, Jenavia Thompson. At birth, I had a broken foot and was deaf in both ears. *As you can tell, the odds were already stacked against me.* My mother is a very strong woman who has complete faith in God and without that, I doubt I would be here today. My first few years in this world were tough. I couldn't hear, and I had a single mother of two children, struggling to make ends meet and she did all of this on public transportation in the late 1970s and early 1980s.

Going back and forth on public transportation was very difficult for my mother because I had a cast on my leg, and it had to be changed every week. Majority of the time, she would have to walk because she didn't have the money to go from Merrick Blvd to Queens General Hospital, which would be two hours. When the cast was changed, they would give her a token to take me back home. This entire process lasted for nine months.

The reason my foot was in a cast was because when I was born, my foot was crooked at a 90-degree angle and they had to break my foot. They told my mother that it would be wise to break it and straighten it out. Being that I was an infant, they said my tissue was still soft and it would heal properly.

In 1979 at the age of three-years-old, I had surgery on my ears for hearing at Mount Sinai Hospital, which at the time, was before modern technology. The doctor asked my mother if she believed in God. *Side note: As you will see, God plays a very important role in my entire life.* My mother said "yes, she does believe in God". The doctor told her that this was a highly complex procedure and if he made one false move, I could be deaf for life and that she needed to pray for me and the surgeons during the procedure.

Being deaf was incredibly difficult because I knew what I wanted to say in my brain, but to verbally communicate it was frustrating. My mother was extremely patient and the bond we had and still have to this day, allowed her to understand me. *I would call it motherly intuition.*

The surgery was a success, but now I have to learn how to communicate. *Like I said, the odds were stacked against me from the start.* At, the age of seven, I took a school bus from 123rd Street to lower Manhattan to attend PS9. The reason I attended this school was due to my speech impediment. They were one of the few public schools that offered speech classes. Every day, I would have speech class with Ms. Barbara Moskoff (*God bless her soul*). The kids in my school were very cruel to me because I was a skinny, tall, dark-skinned kid who could not properly pronounce his words.

Going to speech class was embarrassing because I would have to leave my regular classes, but Ms. Moskoff made me feel very comfortable. She communicated daily with my mother and gave my mother instructions on what exercises to do with me. My biggest issue was that I stuttered, and I couldn't pronounce my L's. Ms. Moskoff taught me how to slow my reaction and take my time before speaking. By the time I entered 4th grade, I no longer needed my speech classes.

My father, Raymond DeWess was a well-known and respected figure in the Islam religious community and a business leader who happened to fall on hard times. My father's downfall came from his love and quest for money and women. To be honest, my father had no presence in my life at all. Occasionally, he would come by and check on me and my mom. One of these times he spent the night, he told my mom the next morning that he was going to get bread, but he didn't come back for three days. Being the strong woman that my mother is, she told him to leave because what he did was wrong, selfish and uncompassionate. This was in 1984 and that would be the last time I saw my father and communicated with him.

Chapter 2: Difficult Decision.

It's 1984 and life is about to became really interesting. My mother, sister and I become homeless this year because our landlord turned out to be a slumlord. As a result, the building we're renting our apartment in was goes into foreclosure. Before this, my mother's family basically disowned her because she introduced my sister and I into practicing African-based religions. They didn't understand why she choose a different path of religion to practice and as a result, they unfairly judged her. *The odds were getting thicker and worst against me.*

Our only hope was my mother's cousin who has access to an abandoned building. He allows us to stay there, even though there is no electricity and only cold water. For the next three to four months, we live in that abandoned building, washing with the cold water. At one point, my mother's cousin figures out a way to run some bootleg electricity into the apartment so that my mom can cook off a hot plate. Despite this, my mother would still go to work every day and my sister and I were still attending school.

My mother is a warrior and her faith in God is rock solid. During this time, she really instills that same belief in me. *I know it was difficult for her, but I thank God every day that I was born to her because these tribulations helped build me into the man I am today.*

So back to the story, my mom makes a huge decision. After speaking with my aunt, with whom my mother had a half-way decent relationship with, she decides to move me in with my aunt in Baisley Projects in Jamaica Queens for the fourth grade. My sister and mother would move in with one of her God-sisters from the spiritual house we attend. The reason being is so that my mom can concentrate on her full-time job while my sister attends high school. I will go to school at PS40. *Note: my speech is still not 100%.* So now I'm 9/10 years old living in the projects in Queens in a two-bedroom apartment with my aunt and my female cousin.

My spot is the couch. I don't have a room and for some reason my cousin who is a huge Michael Jackson fan is extremely mean to me for no reason. *That stills puzzled me to this day.* I'm in an all-new environment and I'm not with my mom every day. I understand why I am in Queens, but it crushes me daily. Oh, by the way, I enter the school at the midpoint of the year, a time when the other kids are situated and there is a rhythm to the energy of their school routines and now here comes this new, complete stranger to the school, myself.

If you know anything about Jamaica, New York and the early 80s, this is the height of the Crack Era i.e.,

Fat Cat, Supreme, and Larry Davis. The crazy part is that I actually seen these dudes and have small interactions with them. (Just a, "Yo shorty. Go to the store for me and keep the change.") They are prominent and respected figures in the Queens 'community and are looked at as celebrities. All the block parties, basketball tournaments, and community events that brought memorable enjoyment moments were funded by these individuals.

Now Back to PS40. My first day of school is in January 1985 and it's snowing. I'm walking to school and make eye contact with a guy who asks me what I'm looking at and I say nothing. He then pushes me into the ground which is covered with snow. This is my "Welcome to Queens" moment. I get myself up and I enter the school. I spend the next six months developing a tough skin and asserting my position. Everyday isn't bad, but it is a challenge because my mom is not around. I'm a new student and I'm stuck in between the neighborhood feuds within the school i.e., New Rochelle, Baisley Projects and Guy Brewer Blvd.

The summer of 1985 is amazing though. I start playing baseball, which I am pretty solid at. Playing skullies in front of the building where you get the push top from the old popsicles and put colored clay in them. The neighborhood jams held on the handball courts were organized by the local drug dealers attended by Run DMC and other hood celebrities.

Chapter 3: Moving On Up.

I get great news. My mom found an apartment in the South Bronx, 172nd and Sheridan Avenue across the street from Taft High School. We would be reunited. I was going from Harlem to Queens to the Bronx. In the Bronx, another crucial, developmental phase of my life happens. My love for basketball and the business of sports from the memorabilia side begins to open up.

Our apartment - 7C - is amazing. It's a huge corner apartment with three bedrooms and one and a half bathrooms. Yep, I have my own bathroom with a toilet and sink in my room. It is also a 15-minute walk from the world-famous Yankee Stadium and Gauchos Gym, both of which would be influential venues in my life. God truly blessed us.

It's now 1986 and I'm 10 years old. My love for baseball goes into another level due to the business side. The apartment buildings have baseball teams that play each other. Within our buildings unofficial team, I play second base and left field and my claim to fame is my defense and hustle. *How ironic is that because little did I know, that would be my key for the rest of my life.*

Life is good. I'm going to school at Columbus Academy which is situated in the building that houses IS 44. Columbus Academy is a program for academically gifted children. Math has always been my strong point. The school consists mainly of well-off children and a few from disadvantaged communities. I play for their baseball and basketball team. Every day I take the C Train from 172nd Street to 81st Street. I'm doing well in school and the spiritual house that we attend unlocks even more levels of God's ability in us.

The Yankees are playing down the street at 161st street. This is before the dynasty starts. These are the Rickey Henderson, Don Mattingly and Ron Guidry days. I start attending professional sporting events by myself. At the time bleacher seats in the old Yankee stadium are only $5 so my mom gives me $10 to get a ticket, soda and a hot dog. I always go early for batting practice. Then one day I overhear some guys talking about how they got autographs before the game. A light bulb goes off in my head, "I can actually meet the guys I'm coming to see play".

For the next two seasons, I collect autographs. In the process, I make a business out of it because certain players sign autographs for the young black kid, especially the visiting teams and that's where I would make money. During the process of getting autographs at Yankee Stadium, I learn what hotels the visiting teams for the Mets and Yankees stay, which was at The Grand Hyatt in Times Square. As a result, I acquire autographs from future All Star and Hall of

Famers such as Cal Ripken, Barry Bonds, Bobby Bonilla, Tom Glavine, Kevin Mitchell, Will Clark (*he was an asshole*) and Frank Thomas. Then I sell them to professional autograph collectors for $50- $100 a piece. I am making some nice money to help my mom out by doing something I love. *This is a common practice till this day.* This is part of the reason why I never sold drugs as a youngster in New York during the crack epidemic.

It's now 1987 and my love for basketball goes to another level because of NY Knicks Rookie Point Guard Mark Jackson. Let me explain. The head priest at the spiritual house my mother and I attend, (*who would be a very monumental figure in my life and my mom's)*, is a former basketball player who during his high school days was the second-best player in New York behind Lew Alcindor. During his time guiding my mother and I, he notices that my interest in basketball is peaking. One day he tells me he has a surprise for me. The surprise is that his Godson has tickets for the Knicks vs. the Chicago Bulls' game. Mark Jackson was killing it at the time, and I had taken a liking to him because of his game and the Nike sneakers he wore. Now I was going to see him play against THE Michael Jordan in person! I *told you, life is good and the odds seem like they are starting to tip in our favor a little.* That night sparks a love of basketball that grows every day since. That summer, 1988, it goes into overdrive when I attend summer camp at Phase Piggy Big on 145th and Nicholas and we are invited to participate in a one-day camp at Gauchos Gym hosted by guess who? Mark Jackson!

The moment I walk up to Gauchos Gym I am in awe. The big Bull's logo on the outside, all their championships trophies on display inside, the photos of all their former players in college or the pros and the fly custom gear that they have at their disposal, especially the jackets. Then bam! As we gather on the court, Mark Jackson walks in. I stand there in complete amazement that I am in the same gym as the NBA rookie of the year. On top of that, when the camp is over, he personally hands out the camp shirts to a few campers and I am one of them. *I told you God plays a big part in my life.* From that day, I was determined to be a part of the NBA as a player or some part.

Chapter 4: Game Changer.

At this point I'm in 7th grade and basketball is my thing. I create makeshift basketballs using aluminum foil wrapped with paper and play imaginary full court games in our apartment, driving my downstairs neighbor crazy. I draw uniforms and different gear and run my own imaginary basketball program (*which later would become a reality.*) Then reality hits and junior high basketball season starts. It's the first time Columbus Academy, my school, has a basketball team so with that being said, we go out and get t-shirts printed. Columbus Academy is stationed in the same building as IS 44 and although we are a totally separate school from them, it causes tension between the two schools.

So, guess who our 1st game is against? IS 44 and some of their team also plays for Gauchos and Riverside Church. *This becomes a clear example of parents know best, but I will get to that later.* That first season we get our asses kicked all year and I mean whipped. We catch 20-point losses on the regular. We play 13 games but win only one. But no matter whether we win or lose, I'm playing hard and hustling, which earns the respect of our opponents and coaches.

The summer before 8th grade, I am approached by a coach to try out for The Riverside Church Hawks. I'm excited but when I tell my mom about the offer she immediately says, "No" and she's very adamant about it. A spiritual reading that she gets from our priest at the time confirms her "no." *In African-based religions readings are important in regard to guidance in your life.* During that spiritual reading, my mom is told that she will be invited to three events and that she shouldn't go to the first or second, but to attend the last. Of course, I'm just 13-years old so I don't care what the reading says. I am just mad and distraught. *Fifteen years later it comes out that, that program and basketball team was a part of the Catholic church sex scandal. I told you God always had my back and my mom had complete faith in God.*

Now it's 1989 and I start 8th grade. The tension between Columbus Academy and IS 44 is nowhere near the same as the previous year because now we have shared lunches and a few classes together along with the sports teams. This was a great decision made by the principals. All is good. Our basketball team is solid, which has brought the entire school together. I'm a little popular, my mom is doing well and spiritually we are rolling well. There is stability and peace. At the end of the school year, I graduate and plan to attend Humanities High School in the fall.

That summer, a life-altering situation happens. My mother has listened to the spiritual reading and skipped the first and second events she's invited to but attends the third, which is an Ogun Akan ceremony. There, she meets the lady who would truly save our lives. They hug each other and cry and it is the start of a lifechanging relationship, and the woman becomes my Godmother. *No matter the odds God always came through for us.* And guess where she is from? Philadelphia.

Chapter 5: P-H-I-L-L-Y.

I'm in 9th grade and throughout the school year my mother and I take weekend trips to Philadelphia to worship at The Sanctuary created by my Godmother, LePeristyle Haitian Sanctuary, is where we receive clarity about why the odds have been against us so far. The weekends my mother doesn't have the money for both of us to go, she leaves me home alone with specific directions on how to cook and take care of myself. At the end of the summer, my mom decides that we should move to Philadelphia to be closer to the sanctuary closer to the sanctuary and get the spiritual help and do the work that we need to reverse the odds against us.

Initially, when we move to Philly we stay with a member of the sanctuary until our apartment is complete. But then the odds turn against us and the storage unit that has our items gets robbed. It's not just clothes and furniture that are stolen, but important documents such as birth certificates, school records, social security cards and other vital documents. This turns out to be a major issue.

On top of that, the job my mom is supposed to start is delayed so we don't even have the money for the deposit on our apartment. The reason for the delay is due to quarterly budgeting and this doesn't shake her faith. She continuously tells me that God is the best planner, and he has never let us down and he won't start now. Our stay at our sanctuary member's house is going to be longer than we thought. Welcome to Philly, The City of Brotherly Love.

The strength my mother has demonstrated though all these obstacles provide me with a strength to acquire success so I can provide and protect her. No matter what has happen, I have never seen her cry or be shaken. Her demeanor is always, no matter what fire is going on, she will find the water to put it out.

It's time for me to enroll in high school which isn't easy since I'm in a brand-new city and don't really know anyone except the guys my age from the sanctuary. *There aren't very many and our interests are different.* The only good thing is I'm at my mother's side and the sanctuary actually has brought clarity and stability to our lives which is crucial. *God is amazing. He will put you through situations to strengthen your faith in him, which in return, makes you stronger spiritually and mentally.* As you can see so far, I have to grow up really quick because everything isn't sweet.

It's the first week of school, but my mom's new job starts at the same time so she can't take me to enroll and they won't allow me to do it without her. It's now the second week, but she can't get time off. Now mind you, we are staying in the badlands of Philly at the time, which is basically a 24-hour open drug market. This shit is like déjá vu all over again. The only difference is I'm with my mom this time. The house we are staying at is far from the best, but hey it's a place to lay our head at and their generosity is appreciated. Being there every day while other people are going to school and work becomes depressing and discouraging.

Finally, my mom gets a day off and takes me to enroll in the local high school. *The odds seems like they are looking good - emphasis on "seems like"*. The school will not allow my mother to enroll me because I don't have any official documentation of who I am. To make it worse, they won't contact my previous schools in New York because they don't know if I am who my mother says I am. *Odds just got worse and it's a wasted day because my mom lost a day's pay. FUCK!!!* It's now October and we are back to square one. Not only do I have to get into a school, but my mom has to find us a new place to live. Thank God for the sanctuary because Sunday service with the beat of the drum and the prayers that are being sung, keep us energized, fulfilled and motivated.

Then one Sunday during late October/early November at service, a member of the sanctuary who heard about the difficulties that I was having with enrolling in school, connects my mother to the original alternative high school in Philadelphia called, Community High School.

Chapter 6: I've Been Though This Before.

Well, let me tell you this. When I say an "alternative" high school, Community was that. It is located in the heart of the badlands and housed in an old warehouse. The majority of students have been kicked out of previous schools for some sort of illegal/violent action or have just come home from a detention center. *Oh boy!* There are maybe 100 students at max in the school and we are required to wear a yellow shirt and navy-blue khakis every day. This is a clear indication of the word "alternative."

As usual, I'm the new guy and my reason for attending the school is totally opposite than 90% of the student body. So now I have to go into PS 40 mentality. *God puts you through certain situations to prepare for you other things that will come up in your future.* I definitely can't let anybody push me to the ground. So, I decide to go into defensive nerd mode aka, be very intelligent but keep to myself until basketball is offered. The problem is that the school is a former warehouse and there is no gym or lunchroom.

Confrontation day finally comes when one of the most feared students who has a serious juvenile record decides I'm being too smart in class. *To this day, I think this is so stupid.* He decides to try me during lunch period. While I'm getting my lunch and walking to my table with the few people I associate with, he decides to call me a derogatory name. "Bitch Ass faggot who thinks he smarter than everybody," he says. Like I said I can't get pushed to the ground again because this is high school not elementary, so I place my tray down and proceed to throw a punch at him that's dead smack on his jaw. Now I'm not going to sit up here and say I won the fight, but I won the respect of the entire school for standing up for myself, especially against this dude who was an actual bully. *Side note: this is the era before guns were commonplace, so a one-on-one fight was just that and nothing more.* We both receive in-house suspension for five days. The crazy part is, that mutual respect is gained, and we learn about each other's backgrounds. Ironically, they are not that different, except the part about violating the law. My reputation in school is now solid.

Guess what happens next? Our vice principal finds a rec center gym not too far away that we use three times a week for student/staff scrimmages. These games are brutal and competitive as shit, but the power of sports is amazing because these games break up different clicks within the student body and creates a healthy mutual dialogue among the staff and students. By February, there is a sense of unity in the school due to the fact when we travel home from school and we interact with the three surrounding high schools that have a lot to say about us. We are forced to stick together, and that's what binds us.

While this is going on, my mom finds us an apartment around the corner from our sanctuary, LePeristyle Haitian Sanctuary. *God works in mysterious ways.* When she informs me of this, I'm happy but not over excited until we I actually see the apartment and where my room is. It was bringing back the same feeling when we moved into our apartment in the Bronx.

That spring, I immersed myself in the Philadelphia basketball scene. This is the era of nationally ranked, K-Swiss sponsored, Simon Gratz, John Chaney Temple Owls, 16th Street, Total Response & Sonny Hill. So everyday, what makes the high school basketball scene unique in Philly is that the results for high school and Sonny Hill are printed in the newspaper on a consistent basis. I find this amazing and very informative.

Also, there was a listing section where tryouts and different events was announced and then one day, I see Northwest Sonny Hill Future League tryouts at Gustine Lake Recreation Center. *That day would be life changing when it comes to my career in basketball.* I go to my mom about the tryouts. Remember the last time I asked her about basketball tryouts was with The Riverside Church Hawks in New York and she said no. This time she says yes instantly with no hesitation. Thank You God.

Chapter 7: Who's The New Guy?

Mind you I'm an outsider when it comes to the Philly Basketball Community. *Odds aren't in my favor to make this team.* I go to an alternative high school that not only doesn't have a basketball team, but it's a school that most people haven't heard of. I haven't played one minute of organized basketball since 8th grade. I've only been living in the city for the past two years and I haven't played for any league or program in Philly. *If you are a gambler, I'm quite sure you wouldn't bet on me making the team.*

Now the day of the tryout is on Tuesday when I enter Gustine Lake. It's a small hot rec center and there is a list that you have to sign for the tryouts, so I do that and then I enter the basketball court area. There are about 40 guys in the gym shooting around interacting with each other and then there is me the outsider. So, I go to the bathroom and change into my shorts, sneakers, shirt and go back out to the court and put my bag in the bleachers and take to the court.

I get up a couple of shots and guys are looking at me sort of weird because no one has any idea who I am and where I came from. Then the coach comes out and blows the whistle and gathers everybody at half court and starts to say everybody's name. Some of the names he announced he's familiar with and jokingly says something about them. Then he gets to Rahim Ali,(that is me, but eventually I changed my last name to Thompson, but I will get to that later), and everybody just looks at me and are very confused, like who is this dude????

So, we go through the normal stretching and drills and I'm not the sharpest when it comes to drills because I haven't been playing competitively except at the park and I'm not at all familiar with them, which leads to some unmemorable moments. I just keep thinking to myself I'm going to get a chance to shine because no matter what I'm not going to quit, I'm going to work hard and hustle.

Then we get to the full courts and this is where I shine and it's not because of offense, it's because of my defense and hustle. My mindset is, "I'm going to be a nag on defense and any loose balls, I'm going after them" and boy did that work in my favor.

The three plays that the coach installed during the early parts of the tryouts, I memorized them. When the opposing team called out the play, my understanding of the play being called, helped my anticipation of where the ball was going. I got three steals in a row and that is what caught the attention of the coach. The coach stopped the play after the third steal and said to the opposing point guard, (who at the time was the best player in the gym), "this guy Ali knows all three plays I installed so can you please think and avoid passing in his direction".

Now the first day of tryouts end and instead of putting your name on a board, the coaches call out who will be returning for the next day of tryouts and guess who's the last name called? Yep, ME! *God has always had my back and I beat the odds that day.*

When I left the gym to take the bus back home, I felt great but there was one problem. The star point guard had an issue with me because I was playing too hard on defense. Whatever!!! I'm thinking to myself, "yep I done created my own niche".

The next and final day of the tryouts is that Thursday, so on Wednesday I replayed all the drills we did and went to the playground to practice them. So, on Thursday, when I get to the gym, it's 20 guys there and there are only 14 spots available for the team.

So, tryouts begin and I'm much sharper during the drills. My passes are crisp, my shots are falling, and I'm very vocal. Then we go into full court scrimmaging and guess who I decided who I'm going to defend, the star point guard, ah damn! I decided to take on the assignment because 1) everybody else was shying away from him 2) I knew this would get me attention 3) if I was going to get cut it wasn't going to be because of effort. Now let's make this clear, he's a bad boy and he can definitely go but I make it hard as shit on him, but I definitely have my moments with a few stops, steals, blocks and deflections. On offense, I'm solid but it's my hustle and defense that stands out.

Then I have my "can't get pushed down moment with him". So, it's game point and it's me and him. Mind you, he's been busting my ass with this hesitation move and I knew he was going to go to this move, so I anticipated it. I steal the ball then pass it to my teammate who misses the layup and they get the rebound and pass it to back to the star PG who leaks up and makes the game winning layup, DAMN! So now it's team decision time and guess who is the 9th pick to make the team? I AM. I'm officially apart of The Philly Basketball Community and I have made The Sonny Hill Northwest Future Stars Team. *I have defeated the odds.*

Chapter 8: Consequences & Fortitude.

Guess what? The program we represent has been dominant for the past few years because the #1 player in the country has played on it and he had now moved on to the Wilt Chamberlain league. Because of this, we will have a target on our back and teams will be seeking revenge due to the havoc the previous teams caused.

Now our practices are competitive, but the Chamberlain team practices were on another level as we saw because they practiced after us. They had the number one player in the country, two all city players and a slew of starters from different strong high school programs across the city. These were the guys who created havoc in the future league and who we were following.

Boy did other teams get revenge on us. It seemed like middle school all over again. The only difference is, I got a lot of playing time due to guys quitting and not showing up for the games after we lost our 1st out of 7 games but then something happened. We won our last four games and gained respect for not folding and when guys tried to return, the coach made the decision not to allow them back.

We started with 14 players and ended with 8 and the kicker part is our best player, the point guard, quit on us after the first of four games and went to another team. And guess what? One of our four victories was against the team he switched to. What made it sweeter was that he barely played because when he came in, we all just attacked him on offenses and defense and went on like a 14 to nothing to run.

Seeing up close and personal all the things my mother went through and how she always kept going no matter what, instilled a "don't quit mentality" in me. *To this day, it has transpired into every form of my life.* So, when we played against my former teammate who quit on us, I took it as a personal offense against my character and everything I stood for.

When the summer ended, I was entrenched and respected by the Philly basketball community and to make it better, I was transferring to Olney High School. Olney has one of the top 50 players in the country. But as usual I was going to be the new guy and have to prove myself again, and for the record, I didn't have a secure spot on the team nor did the coach know I was transferring. They had 8 players returning and there were only 12 spots on the team. *You see a common theme here? I always have to defeat the odds stacked against me, but my secret weapon is my faith in God.*

Now some real live weird shit happens. Our lease at the apartment expires and when my mom goes to renew it, she can't because the property has been sold.

Apartment renting in New York and Philly is completely different. In New York there are a lot of buildings, whereas in Philadelphia, there are a lot of row homes and three floor homes that people turn into duplexes to rent them out as apartments and that's where we were living. That's also why the property was so easily sold.

Now I'm just not going to be starting at another new school, I'm going to be starting at another community to live in. *Odds just tilted a little more against our favor but at this point in my life, I know God has a reason for doing what he is doing.*

A member of our sanctuary had a huge four floor of 31,000sq. *Yes, their place was huge and a FYI the property as of today has been converted into condos. Go figure.* So, for the rent that my mother was paying for the apartment, they gave us half of the first floor with full access to the rest of a house. This was a big-time blessing. *Gods Plan is The Best Plan.* But guess where I'm living now? ...Welcome to North Philly.

North Philly is like a combination of The Bronx and Queens but without the high-rise projects which are replaced by row homes. Instead of the thousands of different people that live in the projects who have six degrees of separation, North Philly has blocks which consist of hundreds of people who all are family and have three degrees of separation. And here I am again, the complete outsider again.

But there is a light of hope and it is around the corner and. That light is Temple University, who at the time has a nationally ranked college basketball program and they have open gym in the evening. *God is amazing because this was a true blessing.*

Chapter 9: Stability.

I get enrolled in Olney High School and started to attend and lol this is not like the Community High School. The actual school is enormous it takes up a full block as a row house would and it has six floors. It must be at least a thousand students in the school. But finally, I have an official schedule of classes and I have gym.

So, the first few weeks of school took some adjusting to but by October, I got a rhythm. At night, I'm playing in the open gyms at Pearson Hall in Temple and I usually get picked. I'm playing against the students and occasionally members of the basketball team which is a hell of an experience meanwhile the high school team is playing in a fall league called Greater Philadelphia and is expected to compete for The Public League Championship.

Tryouts are announced for the high school team for late October and I'm confident I can make the team due to me playing in Sonny Hill and in Pearson Hall. Tryouts come and as usual and I focus on defense and hustle which has become my calling card.

This attribute endears me to the existing team members because they notice all I want to do is win and I'm not coming to take anyone's spot. I'm coming to contribute so when the new members of the team are announced, I'm selected. *I beat the odds again, but I couldn't do it without my source of support, God.*

I'm finally on a winning team and we are ranked Top 10 in the city. Reebok has sent us new sneakers and the whole school is supporting us. I'm a full fledge varsity player and since I'm averaging a whopping 2 points, my name is in the newspaper on a pretty consistent basis which to me is so cool because everybody who scores is included in the Daily News Game Box scores.

On top of that, I became cool with some of the Temple players and they start leaving me tickets to their home games. Home life is stable and I'm becoming even more active in my sanctuary. I get the ultimate Christmas gift, which is that we will be traveling to Virginia to play in a Christmas tournament.

When we get there, we are treated with A1 Hospitality and in the first game, I get extended minutes and boy do I get busy. I score about 8 points in 12 minutes and when the game is over, I actually sign some autographs. *Who would have ever thought I'd be signing autographs?! God is definitely amazing.*

We advanced to the championship game and we end up losing to Germantown Academy (GA), a fellow Philadelphia area school with a star player who ironically committed to the same college as our star player. Honestly, we shouldn't have lost the game but the night before the game, some of my teammates decided to play video games with GA and in the process, they were up extremely late and one of our starters injured his hand in the door playing.

After the lost, there was a lot bitterness and blame among different players on our team (*which would be a foresight to our season*) and to make it worst, we left the runner up trophy in the lobby of hotel. Luckily, one of our assistant coaches went back and got it and still was able to make the train ride back.

I'm going to school every day and playing basketball but there is one problem, I need some money. So, one of the men at my sanctuary, who happens to be my barber, lets me work at his shop by cleaning the barbershop during the week after I'm done practice and all-day Saturday, depending on if I have a game or practice.

This job comes in handy because it ensures I get a haircut on the regular and I have a few extra dollars in my pocket to actually buy some things I like. The really cool thing about this is that I'm able to contribute something to the bills to help lighten the burden on my mom. *God always makes a way.*

The season is going well but there is turmoil amongst the players, which is actually lingering from the season before which I had no idea about. Shit hits the fan after we get thoroughly beat by the number one team in the country, Simon Gratz and then lose at home to the defending Public League champions, Franklin Learning Center *(now closed),* on a buzzer beater.

The next day at practice, the energy is off and then right before practice, one of our seniors informs the team, he is quitting due to favoritism shown by the coach (*WTF*). Now we have to practice. Tempers are high, and patience is low. So, the coach cuts practice short and has us meet in his classroom/ our meeting room.

He goes into a speech about how one person is not bigger than the team, we all have to make better decisions off the court, and no one is exempt from the rules. Myself and a few of the guys are totally confused about where the purpose of this speech is coming from. I'm personally thinking we lost two games to nationally recognized and tested teams, but it's not the end of the world. We still have the rest of the regular season and playoffs. Then the coach says he will see us tomorrow.

When he dismisses us, peep this, the purpose of the meeting wasn't just about the senior who quit. Come to find out, the coach was taking one of our starters, home and that's when a package of crack fell out his pocket and the coach saw it. *Well, I be damn.*

The next day in school is weird as shit and when we get to practice coach inform us that the starter has been suspended indefinitely (*damn*).

Now I know you thinking I am about to step in and be a star player, NOPE, but I do get some increase playing time in the next three games but after that, I'm back to the bench, because its playoff time and he is reinstated. Three wins and we will be playing at the Civic Center (*which is now closed*), in The Public League Final 4. The first two games we win easily but the game to go to the Civic Center isn't as easy. It's a rematch with University City *(now closed),* who we beat earlier in the season.

But this time, their left-handed scoring machine, (*who would later attend Temple University and become one of the best collegiate players in the country*), is coming back for revenge.

Boy does he put on a show and it's not till the last three minutes of the game that we pull away and secure a spot in the Civic Center. I get in for the last minute and a half of the game, lol I have become the human victory cigar and you know what I do when I get in the game? I get the ball and go straight down the lane and make a finger roll lay up the gym goes crazy. I had to make sure my name was in the Daily News the next day.

When the game was over, I was elated. *I defeated the odds again.* I've been in Philly for three years and already played in the Sonny Hill and now I'm going to The Final 4 in the Civic Center. *God really be showing off when you have faith in him.*

The week leading to The Final 4 game is already huge, but the hype is on another level because it's a rematch of us versus the #1 one team in the country, Simon Gratz and it's the #1 player in the country who still is mulling offers from North Carolina and Temple, going against our star player who committed to Villanova. This is big time. TV Stations visit the school, articles are being written about the matchups, the school spirit is popping and I'm all the way a part of it. *God thank you for all your blessings.*

Game day comes and this is totally different because we are playing in a 9600-seat arena and every seat will be filled and the whole city will be watching. When I enter the building, I'm overwhelmed with gratefulness and being realistic. I know we probably won't win this game, but this is the most winning I have ever been a part of along with all the great experiences the season has given me and now I'm playing in the Public league Final 4 in the Civic Center against the #1 team in the country! Something thousands of Philadelphian basketball players have dreamed of but didn't accomplish. *God is AMAZING.*

So, the game starts, and Gratz immediately establishes why they are the #1 team in the country and the 6'11 power forward certifies why he is the best player in the country and will go onto play 16 seasons in the NBA, be a world champion and two-time NBA All Star. He gives a hint of how versatile he is by hitting 2-3 pointers to end the half. *Mind you this is before it was the norm for 6'11 players to shoot the outside moment.*

What made this game extremely better was that even though we lost, this was the first time my mother had actually had the time available to come to my game and from what she experienced she said the people around her was saying, "Rahim should be playing. He would give some energy to the team." And then don't you know, it happens.

I get in with 4 minutes left and I'm hype and my mentality is, "I have nothing to lose because it's the last game of the season". So, we are in a half court set and I get the ball on the wing and immediately beat my defender baseline and attempt a reverse layup and I get fouled and the ball goes into the basket AND 1! You can hear the roars across the audience. The whole Olney section jumps up and cheers!

I feel like I'm the man because my mom saw me score and the crowd supporting me. (*Thank you God. You don't know how much that really means to me to this day, for my mom to witness that moment*). I go to the line and make the free throw. Oh, I'm official like a whistle now. I'm in the scorebook and my name will be in the Daily News. The rest of the game will be a blur and Gratz would go on to win The Public League Championship and end the season as the #1 team in the country across all the national publications. Little did I know, that would be my last official points playing organized basketball. *I will get to that in a few, but you know what, now that I'm older, I couldn't ask for a better way to get my last 3 points.*

Chapter 10: Here We Go Again.

The season is over and it's time for a break after five intense months of classwork, practices, games, and working at the barbershop. So now it's just classwork, open gym during lunch and I got a new job (*boy you won't believe this, but I'll get to that later*). Remember the turmoil I told you about during the season? Well, when the season was over, it finally came to light that a lot of guys wasn't happy with their playing time and how they were used during the season and this came out in our end of the season meeting. This shit was a shock to me because everybody to me played their role to the best of the ability and it's not like we lost to some bum squad. They had nine guys go D1 and the entire roster went to school for free. Oh, by the way for my senior year, I signed up for the work study program (*God always will send you signs, you just have to pay attention*), that would truly come in handy.

So, me being me, I'm like next season is going to be better because this experience will help us and there's a lot of seniors graduating throughout the pub and we have 6 guys returning which includes 3 starters. One who went all pub and one who made honorable mention along with myself, so we should be good. *Boy was I wrong. I'm not talking about in regards about the other guys I'm talking about myself.* So, let me tell you what happened.

Remember earlier when I told you about the Greater Philadelphia Fall League for high school teams, well they have a spring league also. Guess what school was involved? And guess what player didn't know until a JV player asked me, when I was going to play in a game? The crazy part is, when I asked some of the returning players about it, they said all we needed to do was just show up and we will play. So that's what we did and that's when I had my "don't get pushed down moment" with the coach.

So, I get to the game and some of the other returning players are already dressed in their normal #s and then I see one of the JV players with my #31 so when we make eye contact, I immediately tell him to give me my jersey with no problem. I go get dressed and return to the court and now my "don't get pushed down moment" is about to happen with the coach in front of the whole gym.

So, while I'm warming up, the coach comes out and begins to scream at me from across the gym in front of everybody "Son what are you doing here? "Give me my jersey, you didn't earn it. You haven't been to a practice since the end of the season (*and neither has none of the other returning players*), take that jersey off and leave this gym." So now it gets completely silent for 30 seconds and I have my "can't get knocked down moment" in front of the whole gym so I respond, "I'm not your fucking son and who do you think you talking to? Nobody on the team respects you because you show favoritism. I don't need you to be successful in life. Fuck you and this jersey, what kind of grown man are you to scream at me in front of everybody and I have shown you nothing but respect?" As soon as I was done, I took off the jersey and threw it towards the trash can and walked back to the locker room and changed into my clothes. I came back out and watched some of the game and then I left to go to the sanctuary.

When I got to the sanctuary, I told my mom and God-mom what happened. They didn't agree with the language I used but they were glad I stood up for myself because they didn't agree with the way the coach singled me out. Their only advice was be accountable for what I did because I am a young man and excuses aren't acceptable. *As you can see, I was raised by strong Black women.*

So, the next day at school everybody has heard about it. My teammates think I'm crazy, but they agree with everything I said but they said they wouldn't have been bold enough to say it. The senior who quit the team has a newfound respect for me because what I said to the coach, is the reason of why he left the team. Now here comes the irony, my 6th period class shop teacher is guess who? The coach.

So, when I get to class some people are surprised that I'm attending. *(My thinking is why wouldn't I attend. I said it and I meant it. And too be honest, we both were at fault)*, so class goes by and I don't say anything to him, and he don't say anything to me. Then right when the bell rings to end class he asks to speak to me and he says, "your conduct was out of line last night and you will no longer be on the team" so I just look at him and said ok. (*Trust me, I wasn't surprised*).

Guess what I found out the next morning? I found out that I will be going through the last phase of the interview process to get in the Naval Depot Work Study Program. *God's plan is more precise than man's plan*. So, when I go to the interview, I kill it because my academics are in order, I have a prior work history, I have never been in any type of documented trouble. He did however proceed to ask me about the incident with the coach and I explained what happen and he responded by saying, "sounds like to me you had to defend your honor from somebody trying to bully you. I see nothing wrong with that including the language". I was accepted in the Naval Depot Work Study Program.

For my senior year I will work in the morning and attend classes in the afternoon. *God always come through in the clutch*. Now the coach did some shady shit when it came to my grades. I went from a B to a D in his class which absolutely wasn't correct because I turned into all my assignments and never got lower than a C. This was a huge problem because this would have lowered my GPA and that would have affected me in getting into the Work Study program.

When my mother saw this, she immediately arranged a meeting with the principal and the teacher. When we got to the meeting, my mother went directly for the principal's and coach's jugular. When the meeting was over, my grade was changed within 15 minutes. Come to find out, the director of the Naval Depot had seen the drop in grades and was suspicious about the sudden decrease and contacted the principal about it. *God will always have the truth come out and will use the most unlikely person to reveal it.*

Chapter 11: Preparation.

So now I'm set for my senior year. I have a job that can give me some financial independence and I can help lessen the financial burden my mother has. Now let me tell you about my mother's position when it comes to basketball. She supported me playing but her position was "if all these young black boys are getting paid hundreds of thousands of dollars (*this is before the multimillionaire contracts*), what are the owners who are paying them, making?" *This statement would help me in my basketball career and have me start focusing on the business side of the game.*

Remember that new job I told you earlier that I had got towards the end of the season, let me tell you about that. *God will present amazing opportunities to you; you just have to stay focus.* The owners of the house we were renting from, husband asked me if I was interested in having another part time job and I replied, "yes".

He told me to dress nice and gave me the date and address which was located in Center City. So, when I get to the store, I think I'm at the wrong place because it's a jewelry store, but I know this is the correct address he gave me. So, I enter the store and it's all these rings and diamonds in the showcase and I asked for the person who he told me to ask for.

Low and behold, it's the owner of the store who I just saw in a commercial. I'm thinking to myself; this can't be real. He explains to me how he and the owner of the house I live at, were longtime friends who went to college together and he was going to hire me as a favor to him because he heard I was good kid.

Guess what my job will be? I will be a sales associate on Fridays and Saturdays with a set hourly wage and I will get commissions off the wedding bands I sell. *God you are showing off.* And I will start that day by having someone train me. *My employment at this store will cross my path a few years later in the craziest way.*

So, I have a new job and within 2 weeks I'm on my own trying to make sales, now there is a $100 cash pot for those who sells the most diamonds in a day. So, for a month straight I'm killing it and I'm a magnet for couples buying wedding bands. At first it was cute to the staff, but after the second time, it was competitive, and I was no longer the cute young black kid. I was now competition.

So, in case you didn't know, wedding bands sales are a seasonal thing with a focus on the springtime. In the short period of time that I worked there, I made some really good money and then right after the school year ended, I was told they didn't need me for the summer season due to my position being seasonal. I'm convinced my dismissal was due to the rate of sales that I were acquiring, and I know for a fact there was some jealousy from some of the staff towards me. Little did I know, this wouldn't be the last time me and the jewelry store owner's family will cross paths. (*Later on, I will talk about this beacuse it's very significant. God's will is very interesting*)

So now we are at the summer before my senior year. I'm not playing in Sonny Hill League but remember, I love the game, so I attend a lot of the Hill League games and, in the process, I discover The North Central Philadelphia Basketball League aka 16th and Susquehanna.

But before we get to that, just because I'm not playing varsity basketball and not playing in the Hill league that doesn't mean I've stopped playing. Remember I've been playing at Pearson Hall in Temple since we moved to North Philly and now it's the spring/summertime and I'm competing everyday among college students and solidifying my relationship with the Temple's men's team. What made this so monumental is that the Temple team had just made an Elite 8 run in the NCAA Tourney and would be a pre-season Top 25 team.

That summer is basically a basketball internship for me because I'm starting to know all the influential players in the Philly basketball community, rather they were a league director, player, coach, scout, agent, score bookkeeper, ticket scalpers, gamblers, fanatics, etc. This is very good for me because I'm starting to create a network of individuals to follow and learn from. Then one day, I had an unexpected, "don't get knock down moment" with my ex assistant coach from the Sonny Hill Future league.

So, one day he sees me at a game, and he asks me what I'm going to do now that I'm not playing ball anymore. Now this is my 'can't knock down moment" because I didn't expect him of all people to ask me a shallow question like that. I tell him, "I'm going to create a basketball league one day". He looks at me and laughs and then says "that can't happen. Sonny Hill league is the only league for the real players". I looked at him in shock and then I responded, "watch me" and I walked away. *God will put you in certain positions to piss you off and make you work harder.* Little did he know he added more fuel to my fire and guess where I was on my way to? The NCPBL Games aka 16th Street and boy would that be a game changer.

Before I get to that, I know you're probably thinking, he's playing and is around all this basketball but how is he making money because we know is mom isn't doing that well financially and he's a 17-year-old, so where is he getting money from? *Lol, even though you might not be thinking that, I'm going to tell you anyway.*

I was dismissed from the jewelry store in late June. At The Naval Depot Work Study Program, the work part started in August so that we can have paid training in what duties we will be performing, but I still had a nice amount of money saved from the Jewelry story. *I would give half my commission money to my mom for bills and I would save the other half and I'm glad I did. Thank God. FYI, you know the voice you hear in your head that tells you to do something. LISTEN TO IT!*

That summer at Sonny Hill League there was a 6 foot 6, bald headed kid from Italy, that was the son of a former NBA Player who had returned to the area and killing everybody he plays against and he's doing it in LA Gears and High Socks. We will get back to him and this story later.

So now back to 16th Street. This was something unlike I had ever seen in a person before. It was outside basketball, but it was like a block party. There's a live DJ and you can smell fried fish in the air, the aroma of the weed smoke, the pretty women and the dope boys walking by, rimmed out automobiles, people gambling, and basketball is the center of attention of it all. This is Will Smith's song "Summertime" in the flesh. This energy was amazing.

So, my summer schedule was officially set. Pearson Hall runs from 11am-2pm back home from 2:30-4:30pm Sonny Hill from 5-8pm and 16th Street runs from 9-11pm. 16th Street was off the chain. Sonny Hill was where all the top high school and college players, played and the 16th Street teams were funded by the local entrepreneur urban pharmacists with the hood basketball legends who just didn't stay focused, sprinkled with some of the top college players who are sneaking to play. *This was before social media.*

This was a different sector of basketball that I wasn't used to, and I loved it. So, let me tell you about a certain college player sneaking to play lol. There was a certain left-handed shooting guard who played in the NBA for 10 years, went to an Atlantic 10 Conference school and his mother didn't want him to play in that "atmosphere". *It's no way that can happen in this time of day.*

Chapter 12: Training.

Now Philly is a city of style and fashion and in the 90s, it's on a whole another level and 16th Street makes that clear with the rims on the car, the colored polo clothes, fresh sneakers and cuts. Remember this is the era of the drug dealers as the hood icon, more than the rappers or athletes.

So, I take some of the money I have saved and really start to pay attention to my wardrobe and boy oh boy I get busy. I find out that Ross Outlets has authentic Ralph Lauren Polo at a discount rate and boy did I rack up. I got four polo collared shirts along with shorts, polo socks and white polo t-shirts, a few pairs of Reebok classics and Air Force 1s. On top of that, I'm about to start working in August. Oh yea, I'm rolling.

When I attend the games, I always got a fresh cut and I'm Polo'ed down from head to toe. (I do a great job mix and matching my four outfits along with the socks and white tees) and to put the icing on the cake, I'm about to start working. So now when I attend games, I'm noticing I'm getting more attention from the ladies they are laughing a little more at my jokes and the basketball players are being more interactive with me.

Now I'm a regular at 16th Street and I'm tapping into a different area of the basketball culture. *God will have you cross paths of people from all different walk of life that have the same interest you have.*

My basketball "internship" reached another level when the two Temple basketball stars makes USA Basketball and win gold medals. This raises the profile of the university entering the college basketball season and the players are projected NBA 1st round picks. My fashion style gets the attention of one of them and now I am his unofficial young boy, (*this would carry a lot of weight*).

August comes and now my senior year officially starts when I begin at the Naval Depot Work Study Program. But before I get into that let me tell you what's going on with me at my sanctuary.

The messages for me are coming from the Loas via readings and possessions about being a leader and having the ability to help make a change in people's lives. I can actually believe and see me accomplishing that because of the different connections I'm gaining and the statement my mother made about, *who are the owners of the teams, is starting to make sense to me.*

Since we moved to Philadelphia, I have never missed a Sunday service but it's different because now that I'm 17, I'm actually going because I want to, and it doesn't feel like a chore/requirement. So, during services I'm paying attention to the dances and becoming more better at and when the Loas (Holy Forces), come in possessions. *You know in the Church when somebody says the person is touched by the Holy Spirit well, in African based religions, Priests are trained and used for the Loa to possess on them and give a message to the to help protect and uplift people.* During the drumming and singing they bring me out to dance and it seems to energize the service.

So, all these trials and tribulations that I been though in my young life are producing some good results and my faith in God is becoming stronger because I actually believe I can make my dreams a reality due to all the blessings God has already granted me.

So, my senior year schedule is: wake up at 6:00am and leave house at 6:30am to catch train and bus from North Philly to the Naval Depot in the Northeast. Work starts at 8am and ends at 12pm. My job is to fulfill naval depot students' textbook orders, so I would get 40-50 orders a day and a single order can be as small as 5 books and could be as large as 50 books. Then from 1-4pm we have school which consist of Economics and English. I would do my homework on the bus/train ride home. Then I would get home by 5:30pm.

Soon as I get home, I would leave out to play at Pearson Hall and then go to their cafeteria to eat. The best nights were game night at McGonigle Hall for the nationally ranked Temple University basketball game. Now let me tell you about McGonigle Hall. The building only holds 3900 people, and it would be packed past capacity lol and I know this for a fact because I personally know people who snuck into games.

The Temple games was the "IT" place to be because they were Top 25 in the country, they had a Hall of Fame head coach, and two All Americans who was projected to be NBA 1st round picks. Guess who was at every home game and name was on the will call list? I was, and it was like a badge of honor because it was only 3900 assigned seats for a nationally ranked team.

For game day I would always make sure I looked good, my outfit and sneakers were crisp, my haircut sharp, and I had a few dollars in my pocket. *Remember I'm in work study.* I would arrive to the McGonigle hall for game night and it would be lines and crowds of people and I would bypass all of that and go up to the will call window, *(God is getting me ready for what lies ahead of me)* and say my name along with the person who left the ticket for me. I had three players who would take care of me. I would receive my first ticket and walk into the game. *Damn that felt so good even to this day.*

When I would enter to go to my seat, it was in the section behind the Temple bench. This section was like a who's who of Temple Basketball i.e., players' family members, alumni, former players, donors, respected and well-known individuals, etc., and I'm sitting amongst them as an equal. *God is preparing me for what my life will consist of later on.*

By the third home game which is a nationally televised game against top 10 Cincinnati, my rhythm and routine is in place. The people in my section know I'm a regular and when they find out I'm a high school senior who doesn't play varsity basketball, who works at the Naval Depot (*which was a huge deal at the time*) and is cool with the entire Temple Team and the future conference player of the year/NBA draft pick, considers me his young boy, people started looking at me differently and treating me with more respect. Now I'm starting to get an elementary understanding of the business of basketball.

Chapter 13: What Does The Future Hold?

Life is good but through all of these experiences, I haven't applied to college yet. So, one day I asked my teacher at the Naval Depot about applying to college and he looks at me with an odd look and asked me, "why haven't I done that already? What advice did my guidance counselor give me and why didn't my high school coach tell us about the process?" I responded back, "Honestly I don't know and what is a guidance counselor?" He then asked me if I had taken the SATs. I then respond, "When will you be giving them?" He then realizes that I had no type of idea about the college admission process.

He then goes on to explain to me about college application fees, SAT testing dates and fees, gathering my academic transcripts, etc. (*God bless this man because he always took time to give me knowledge*). He then asks me what colleges I'm interested in attending and I tell him Temple and I explain why. Come to find out, he's a Temple alumnus. He tells me to gather all the information and get back with him. *The odds have gone against me again.*

So, the next day, (*remember this was before the highway information was invented aka the internet*), after school instead of going to Pearson Hall, I find out where I can get a Temple admissions application from. Come to find out, one of the guys who I played with during the Pearson Hall open gyms, worked in the admissions office and thought I was a student there. *FYI come to find out I should have never been allowed in Pearson or the cafeteria.*

He then gives me the information I need. When I look at the application, it's like reading at a foreign language. I then seek out information about the SATs which isn't as easy but finally after about two weeks, I get the date and the price of the test. Now remember, time is going by and it is getting later in the year and I'm thinking the SAT is a regular math and reading test, but boy was I wrong.

So, I gather the information and fill out the application as best as I can. It's now late January, early February and I get the information to my teacher one day during lunch and he reviews what I have written and lets me know this isn't going to be easy and that I have a lot of errors. *When he tells me this, I'm very discouraged.*

So, he tells me he is going to take it home and see what he can do. The next day he comes back and while I'm at work I get summoned to his class. He then shows me what he has done and also provides me with a confirmation date for the SAT test in March. (He paid for it but when I get my check, I have to give it back to him in my next check). He then informs me that I can't send the application off until I do my essay, explaining why I should be accepted in Temple.

He lets me know I won't be working for the rest of the week and my focus should be on completing the essay so I can mail out the application before the final deadline. He really took an interest in my success, so I said ok. By the end of the week, it's complete and we send it off. Mind you, I'm still attending Temple's basketball games and they are now a Top 10 team in the country and access to their games are at a premium level.

The business side of basketball is really starting to kick in with me, as Temple ascends to a Top 10 team. The values of home game tickets have increased and what made it more valuable is there is only 11 home games for the year and it's only 6 home games left. So instead of asking for one ticket I ask for two, and with the second one, I would sell it. Boy oh boy this would increase my financial status.

So, my old head, (*the future A10 player of the year and first round draft pick*), ticket requests have increased so I don't even approach him about a second ticket. I go to my other two guys and they tell me it's no problem because they don't have family in the area and that shouldn't be a problem.

Now remember I told you earlier I was meeting and getting to know all the influential figures in the Philly basketball scene? There was one ticket scalper who also happened to be a coach in the Sonny Hill League and was well respected at the 16th Street games, who also happened to live in my North Philly neighborhood, who recognized me attending the

Temple games. So, when I got the second ticket, that's who I went to about selling it.

So, one day it's a Saturday noon ESPN game and I get there early as usual and I see him. I walk over to him and let him know I will have a second ticket for the rest of the home games, and I want to sell it. He looks at me like what? Mind you, they top 10 in the country with now two, 1st round locked in NBA draft picks. I then tell him if he can sell the second ticket which is behind the Temple bench and right next to me, we will spilt it 50/50. *I've always been fair when it comes to the business because I want the business to continue.*

That day and the rest of the season, he sells the second ticket for $100 and I get an additional $50 before I walk into the game on top of whatever money I already had or didn't have. *The business of basketball is starting to become embedded in me.*

Now as the NCAA tourney approaches, it's time for me to take my SATs. Plain and simple this is a total disaster when I get there. I'm not prepared or confident that I will do well. When we begin the test, I don't know shit. *I know you're thinking, why didn't he take the PSAT? Shit I'm thinking the same thing.* This was the longest three hours of my life. When I walked out of there, I knew I didn't do well.

Temple was eliminated in the second round of the tourney and graduation is three months away. By the way, I was denied admission to Temple and my SAT score was a 680. Imagine if I actually studied and was prepared for the test. So now I have a dilemma. Where will I be going to college is my question, but on the bright side, I've been picked by the Naval Depot to work through the summer.

A member of my sanctuary, (*as you can see the sanctuary is the stable rock in my life*), suggests I apply for Community College of Philadelphia being that their tuition is inexpensive plus I would be eligible for financial aid. I can attend there and then transfer to a 4-year school as long as I take the correct classes and the icing on the cake was that CCP accepts everyone. It looks like I'm going to be a college student!!!!!!

So, I get the application and apply and by the time we start graduation practice in June, I've been accepted as a non-matriculated student, meaning I will be attending CCP in the fall but before I take College 101 classes, I have to take 098 classes due to the fact that I didn't have the right amount of college preparation in my English and math classes. Hey, it's cool with me. Whatever needs to be done, I'm willing to do it and I'm built to do it because my life has consisted of beating the odds.

June comes, and I graduate but before we move ahead, one night, me and a few of homies went to the movies to see "Above the Rim" featuring 2Pac.

This movie is amazing to me and it shows another side to the basketball industry, which I'm familiar with due to the games at 16th Street but seeing something on the movie screen similar to what I actually attended, added more motivation for me to succeed in the business of basketball.

Chapter 14: Getting Ready.

So now I'm 18 and I'm a freshman at CCP. I have
gotten a job at the School bookstore which I work at
four hours a day. I have my English 098 class from
8-9am, my Math 098 class from 9:15-10:15am and I
go to the gym from 11am-12:30 pm. After the gym, I
work at the bookstore from 1pm-5pm. From work, I
go home and then I go to Pearson Hall to hoop in the
evening.

I'm still dealing with Temple University Hoops
Program even though my old head graduated and was
already drafted. The other two guys I deal with on the
team are still there. So, freshmen year comes and it's
not that eventful. The Temple basketball team isn't
nationally ranked, but they make a late February run to
get into the NCAA Tourney.

But there is one moment that God shows me that my
future in the business of basketball is going to happen.
It's January 1995 and the Lakers will be playing
against the 76ers at The Spectrum (*which is now
closed*). My Old Head, who used to play for Temple,
had been drafted by the Lakers that spring. During that
summer he told me he would have a ticket for me

when they come to play the 76ers and for me not to worry about it.

Now let me explain something to you. Since we moved to Philly in 1990, I have probably been to maybe five NBA Games and my sports memorabilia business wasn't as booming as it was in NY due to the fact of my commitment to playing basketball. *But I still knew what hotels the visiting teams stayed at and I would have a memorable moment with one of the most iconic figures in basketball history, but I will get to that later.*

Now back to the Lakers 76ers Game so it's a Saturday afternoon and since I knew what hotel the visiting NBA teams stayed at, (The Sheraton in Society Hill), I decided to go to the hotel to double check with him that I had a ticket for the game that night. Well, there is a loop thrown in this plan.

Just so you know there are two buses for NBA teams. One would leave at 3:30-4pm which is mainly the coaching staff, support team and the non-rotational players and the second Bus would leave at 4:30/4:45pm and that would be for the stars, starters, and rotational players.

So, I know I have to get to the hotel by 3:30pm but when I get there, I don't see any Martz buses or people seeking autographs. Now I know that I'm not late, so I asked one of the Doormen who I was cool with, "what's going on"? He said, the Lakers are staying at the Marriott by the airport.

Now to get to the Sheraton was easy on public transportation. I would take the Broad Street Line to City Hall and take the El to 3rd Street and then walk over to the hotel. To get to the airport was not easy at all. Plus, it required two buses on top of taking the trains.

Now it's no way I can make it to the airport in time for the buses, so I decide to grab something to eat and go on down to the Spectrum and prayed to God that I get into the game.

The odds aren't looking that good right now, I haven't heard from the Old Head since the summer, the hotel where the teams normally stay at isn't the one for this game and I don't know anything about the will call process for an NBA game at the Spectrum.

So, I get down to the Spectrum which is totally different from going to a game at McGonigle Hall because I don't know anyone and that same confidence that I have for Temple Games is gone. I'm in a whole new environment (*sounds familiar?*).

So, when I walk to the arena from the subway it's around 5:30pm so I know both buses have already arrived. I see a security guard and I ask where the players will call is and he directs me to the steps I have to go down to get to the window.

As I walk down the steps, I'm praying to God I hope my name is on the list. So, I enter the will call area this is totally different from what I'm used to, whereas in

McGonigle, the will call was in the lobby of the hall. This will call is separate from the entrance to the arena.

The security guard immediately approaches me, not imposing at all and asked me which team I was here for. I tell him the Lakers and he directs me toward the window where their tickets are being distributed at.

I stand in line and there is about 4 people in front of me and then it was my turn. The Mailbox office attendant says, "Hello are you, what is your name and the player who left them for you?"

I respond "My Name is Rahim Ali and ??? left them for me"

The Attendant then says "Please give me ID"

So, I pass my College ID to him.

He then takes it and checks the mail rack where the tickets are left in envelopes.

He then returns and says he doesn't see my name because all the tickets haven't come up yet and to stand over there with the other people who are waiting. *It's about 12-15 people waiting so I am feeling good about my chances.*

So about 10 minutes later he announces all the Lakers tickets have come up and for all those that have been waiting, please get back in line.

Now at this point the crowd has grown to almost 50 people waiting for their tickets, so they opened up another window. I get back in line with the attendant who I previously interacted with. So, when I get to the window and give him my ID he goes check and comes back and says he doesn't see no tickets for me (*damn*).

So, I then respond, "Are you sure?" He then asks me would it be under another name I then say, "it might be under Young Boy" he looks at me oddly and then I said, "that's what he called me his entire time at Temple".

The attendant then says he's going to call the locker room and speak to the equipment manager who is in charge of the tickets after he is done with everybody else in the line behind me. And for me to stand-off to the side.

Now I am thinking this is not going to happen and today was a complete waste of time and it's almost 6:30pm and the game starts at 7pm. Then the attendant says "Young Boy come to the window" over the PA System.

I then walk up to the window and the attendant tells me the Equipment manager wasn't able to speak to my "Old Head" and there is no ticket left for me, but if there is an extra ticket available for the game and he will give it to me. *Faith even in the bleakest situations, will help you.*

I get the ticket and then I go enter the arena. *The lesson I learned from this was, always reconfirm with people when they say they are going to do something for you*. By the way, the 76ers won that night but my "Old Head" almost got a poster on the 7'6 Center from the 76ers and in case you were wondering, I never asked him for tickets again.

1996 would be the year I officially embark on my journey in the business world of basketball.

Chapter 15: Opportunity.

Now before I get to that I'm now a full-time matriculated student at CCP (*this would be very interesting*) because I have passed my 098 and 099 classes. My High school teammate who plays for Villanova University and I had reconnected at the Nova-Temple game the year before and ironically Villanova is now nationally ranked, and he is leaving me tickets for the games they play in the city.

Oh, by the way we have moved out of the house we were staying at to around the corner to an apartment on the 3rd floor of a brownstone with our own separate entrance, a deck, 2 bedrooms, Kitchen,1 bathroom and a living room.

Now I know you are thinking, what's going on with Temple and me? While all the guys who I was cool with have all graduated and now that I'm attending CCP and working my time is now nonexistent at Temple Basketball Games and Pearson Hall.

One night I'm at the sanctuary and I'm doing my homework and my God mom walks by me and says when am I transferring from CCP I tell her that I have to complete another year at CCP before I can transfer to a 4-year school and she just gives me a look.

Then another day comes, and she asks me again and I tell her the same thing again. *Mind you, my Godmother, Gro Mambo Angela, is a world renowned famous respected psychic* and this time she tells me, just apply to the schools, you don't know what is going to happen.

So, the next day I go to the college admissions and guidance office at CCP. I got a few applications to some local and state universities but there is one that stood out and it's for Night School at Drexel.

So, I decide to apply. This time unlike the time I filled out the Temple Application I was confident in filling it out and the criteria they were asking for I was able to provide it.

Now remember it's 1996 and the two most popular basketball players are Allen Iverson at Georgetown and Michael Jordan of the 72-10 Chicago Bulls and I'm blessed to have interactions with both of them.

It's February 1996 and my former teammate who plays for Nova leaves me a ticket for their ESPN Big Monday Game at The Spectrum versus Georgetown University led by Allen Iverson. Now I go to will call and there is a Villanova table set up for those receiving tickets.

I go up and say my name and I receive my ticket with no problem unlike the last time I was there for the

Lakers-76ers game. I get my ticket and when I walk in my seat is immediately behind the nova bench and I also have a post-game pass (*this is new to me and would expose me to another aspect of the basketball business*).

This game is one of those games that if you are a hoop fan, you wanted to be at. I haven't felt this energy since The UMass-Temple Game in 94 but this different, it's 19 thousand fans on Big Monday with Dick Vitale announcing the game between two historic Big East Rivals and 7 Future NBA Players playing along with a Future Hall of Famer.

This game is unbelievable. Iverson is showing why he's the best player in college basketball and The Nova Team is showing why they are a top 25 team after almost a decade of non-relevance and my high school teammate is out there balling.

Somebody I actually played with is on one of the biggest stages in college basketball, performing at a high elite level versus a traditional college power. This is a WOW moment for me.

Nova ends up winning the game and now I need to find out what this Post game Pass is for. So, I ask the usher from my section and he points me to a tunnel that leads to the hallway of the locker rooms. I play it cool but I'm thinking this is big time access. *God will show you and have you experience certain things just so that you can get used to them, but at the same time, never take them for granted because you know it's a privilege.*

So, this is a new experience for me. I never did this at any Temple game I ever attended. So, I'm standing there and WOW, the announcers are walking past the coaches and then the Georgetown players start to come out and low and behold Iverson comes out literally right behind me and I make it a point to tell him he's a bad boy and his future is bright as shit. He stops and looks at me and says, "thanks homie, that means a lot." *(Little did I know this wouldn't be my first of many interactions with him)*. He was then whisked away to the bus by Georgetown security *(ironically this wouldn't be my last interaction with the Georgetown program either)*.

Then the Villanova team came out and my high school teammate was among them and we talked briefly. I let him know how proud of I was to see him on this big stage playing the way he did. The whole nation now knows who Olney High School is. That night I left the arena, I was more determined than ever to get involved in the business of basketball. I just have to figure out how.

Meanwhile, the biggest thing in pop culture is The Chicago Bulls aka the Rock stars, Michael Jordan, Scottie Pippen, Dennis Rodman, Triangle Offense, Breakfast club, Zen Master,72-10. Possibly best team ever, Chicago Bulls.

So, every basketball fan in the world is following them because they are champions, and they are doing it with style, flash and substance. But there is one name that I notice every time you read about Michael Jordan and his off-court business and that name is David Falk, his agent.

I go on a mission of getting his office contact information, this is the era of hard copy research way before the world of Google Search. So, I go to the library and get the Washington DC Yellow pages because I have found out that's where the business FAME is located. So, I began a letter writing campaign trying to get an internship or job with him. And yes, I did say letter writing campaign and I will get back to that later.

So now we are entering Mid-March and The Chicago Bulls are coming to town now the ability to get tickets is out of the question because of what the price point was but the ability to see them live wasn't.

Now as I told you previously the teams would stay at The Sheraton in Society Hill or The Marriott by the Airport. The reason being is that they were convenient to arena The Marriott was a 10-minute ride at the most and Sheraton was 20 minutes and that included traffic.

I'm thinking to myself I have to find out what hotel they are staying. *So, before Academy Buses was the official transporter of the teams, it was Martz Bus-line.*

Chapter 16: Determination.

I go to the yellow pages and call the bus line and tell them I'm double checking the arrival of the Chicago Bulls team bus to the Sheraton in Society Hill hotel the operator who answered the phone tells me I'm mistaken, and they will be staying at the Four Seasons Hotel on the Parkway. I immediately hang up and I'm hype as shit.

Now when the Bulls would travel to an opposing team city, it was a major event. The news media would film their every move from the arrival on the plane to the hotel to arena to their departure from the city. Whoever was somebody rather they were a celebrity, athlete, politician, hood figure, etc., would be in attendance at the game.

That Monday, it's game day and I decide not to attend class because I'm going to hotel and get a chance to meet Michael Jordan and the Bulls in person.

I get to the hotel at 1:30pm. Boy oh boy, everybody must have called the bus company to find out where they are staying because it easily 100 people in front of the hotel wearing Bulls apparel with different items wanting to get signed. This is definitely not going to be an easy task and on top of that besides the normal hotel security, they also have police officers to help control the crowd.

I'm thinking how I will get close enough to Michael Jordan to get at least a good picture reminder. *This is before camera phones, so photos were even more valuable.* I only had three items with me, a disposable camera, sharpie marker and the entire Chicago Bulls Basketball team basketball cards in a card case.

As time goes by the crowd get less and less and by the time 3:30pm comes, there may be 20-25 people left. Some people had to go back to work, some just left, I'm thinking to myself this is perfect the odds for interaction is looking better. Then the two Martz Buses pull up its almost showtime.

It's now probably 3:45/4pm and members of the Bulls traveling party start coming out the hotel and boarding the bus. Then Dennis Rodman comes out and immediately enters a regular vehicle and departs. Right after him Randy Brown exits, and he signs for me then a few more players come out none of them sign for me except for Jud Buechler.

Now I'm doing a mental count. Mike nor Phil has come out and there are at least another 4 more players left. Then it happens. Legendary, Bulls security guard, John Capps exits out, so I know for a fact MJ and Pippen is coming out. When Capps come out, he immediately makes a stiff arm to the autograph seekers to his left and low and behold it's MICHAEL

JORDAN in a three-piece suit and a derby hat with a shoulder bag looking like a busy businessman

I just happen to be on the right side away from the other autographs seekers and I walk up to him and I'm not even thinking about an autograph, I just want a picture which especially in that era would be a moment from that day. Plus, I didn't pick up the vibe that he was going to sign because he was moving quickly.

I asked him "Mr. Jordan can I shake your hand and take a picture please he looked at me and shook my hand and said hurry up and I snapped a pic with my disposable camera!!!!! *FYI, I had to prepare the camera for this pic in advance because in those days, you had to roll the dial till it stopped so that you can take a pic and I had mine ready.*

I was hype as shit because he didn't stop for anybody else and in a blink of an eye, he was on the bus. Traffic that was passing came to a stop when they realized it was MICHAEL JORDAN. *This would be the only time I ever meet him.* I then turned around and Scottie Pippen had on sunglasses, a long trench coat buttoned up and walking towards the bus. He doesn't respond at all when I ask for a picture. Phil Jackson is a few feet behind Scottie and he clearly says, "I'm not signing no autographs or taking pictures please let me get to the bus".

They all board the bus and depart for the game. I feel good as shit because I beat the odds again and met Michael Jordan, the most famous athlete in the world.

Now, me on the other hand I have about 9-10 pics left on my disposable camera and I can't get this film developed unless the whole roll is done so on the way home, I take a bunch of bullshit pics so the roll can be complete, and I can get it developed at the local Rite Aid.

When I get home, I immediately go to the Rite Aid that's in my neighborhood and give them the roll to get developed which would take 2-3 weeks basically April. Now I have even more motivation in my David Falk, letter campaign, to work for him

That April, two great things happen. I get my photos back that have Michael Jordan in it, and I was accepted to Drexel University Night School Program, beginning in June 1996. *This is a total surprise and shock to me.* I will be taking two 3-hour classes on Monday and Thursday and I will have to meet with the guidance counselor on a certain date to discuss which classes I will be taking and what financial payment options I have. The icing on the cake is, Drexel just beat Memphis in the NCAA Tournament, so the basketball program now has a national profile.

That night, I let my God Mom know what happened about getting into Drexel. She smiled at me and said, "what I tell you?". *From this moment on, I never hesitated to do anything that she told me to do and you will see this later on in my story.* When I told my sister, she was taken back because she worked in the education system and never heard of a Community college student getting accepted to a 4-year university on any terms before completing all of their community college requirements. *God has always positioned me for success.*

Chapter 17: Reality.

Life is stable and going good. We have secured housing, spiritually we are grounded, I've going to school every day which is where I also work. In regard to basketball, I'm attending nationally ranked Nova games along with having and reading Slam magazines on the regular. I have a subscription, so now I am up to date on everything happening in the culture of basketball.

During that time, Slam magazine is new and there are 10 issues, and I have become an avid reader since the Shawn Kemp cover because they are different than Street and Smith, Sports Illustrated and Hoops Digest.

They are Hip Hop aka urban with their style of writing along with the photos and they are covering the culture of basketball from the playground to the NBA along with the style and fashion that comes with it. And what made it so dope and rare, was that it only came out every 2-3 months.

Since I worked in the bookstore, I would always be able to get the magazine as soon as it came out. So, the new issue comes out for May and it's early April.

Jerry Stackhouse is on the cover, who is playing for the 76ers at the time. I get it and read it cover to cover and towards the back I see an ad that says, "Slam Magazine is looking for promotion reps in different cities to promote Slam Magazine at different basketball related events".

I immediately take that part out of the magazine and complete the process which consisted of writing a cover letter explaining who you are and why you should be picked, along with a resume of your basketball experience. I'm on it. *This is way before email and laptops, so I had to type the letter on a typewriter and physically mail it.*

This is the chance I've been waiting for! I know if I get blessed with this opportunity, I can go very far with it and at the current time it would solidify me as a business figure in the Philly basketball community and not as a player. I was determined to be respected as a business figure and not a former basketball player.

I knew the odds of me playing collegiate basketball was very slime but my chances of entering the business was much better I know but it would be more difficult because the path is different, and I didn't have a blueprint. Now besides the David Falk Letter Campaign, I now have the Slam Promo Opportunity that I'm seeking I'm determined to get in the door of the business of Basketball.

It's now June and I have started my two-night classes at Drexel and I'm no longer at CCP. I have a job in the morning and then I would go to campus in the afternoon to hoop in the gym and get acquainted with the campus.

Side note, my God mom has arranged a family vacation to Disney World in Florida, mind you this is in 1996. This will be very significant, and I will explain that very soon.

One day I come home and there is a letter in a manila envelope from Slam in my room and I'm nervous and hype. I open it and I begin to read the letter. OH SHIT! I've gotten the promo position as a Slam rep in Philly. I'm in the door, *(thank you God)*! At the end of the letter it says, "If you interested in becoming an integral part of our team please contact us at this number". Are you kidding me, shiiiittttttt!

The next day I call the number and speak to the Director of National Promotions and he says he's glad to hear from me and that I accepted the position. I tell him that I'm honored to be picked *(meanwhile I'm thinking I made my lane in my Philadelphia basketball community, which I would continue to do)*. He lets me know he will be sending me magazines, stickers, posters, a banner and a few shirts in the next few weeks which would be the end of my first quarter at Drexel and the time being me going on family vacation and this would be significant. So, the family vacation comes, and this is the first time I had ever been to Disney. Their slogan "The Happiest Place on Earth", would definitely apply to me within a few days. Let's get to it.

On the way to Disney, I'm flying with my aunt who happens to be an Irish woman and while we are in the airport, I see Maurice Cheeks who's on the same flight as us. I stop him to ask for his picture and his opinion on Allen Iverson, who the 76ers just drafted as the #1 pick and was all the hype warranted? He replies, "He's going to be better than me". *This vacation as you can see, is also becoming a business trip.*

MJ has returned for a full season in the NBA and the Bulls have the best record ever in the NBA 72-10 and start their 2nd 3peat. The big story of the basketball summer was that the second installment of the Olympics' Dream team would be playing in Atlanta, headlining by the new NBA Super Duo of Shaq and Penny along With Scottie Pippen, Charles Barkley, Hakeem Olajuwon, Reggie Miller, Gary Payton, Mitch Richmond, John Stockton, Karl Malone, David Robinson and Grant Hill. The other big story of the summer is the free agency of Shaq, who currently plays for the Orlando Magic.

I would read the newspaper every day and while we were on vacation. It was no different than any other day. Then one day, I'm reading the Orlando newspaper and they are talking about Shaq impending free agency decision rather he would return to the Lakers or stay with the Magics. The irony is, he's on the Olympic team and they are practicing in Orlando at The Disney Wide World of Sports Complex.

So, me being who I am I contact the Director of National Promo at Slam and let him know I'm in Orlando and the USA Team is practicing down here and I'm going to attempt to get a media credential using my Slam Promo Position. He tells me go ahead and if I need any verification, have them call or fax him.

That night when we return from Orlando, I let my Godmother know what I'm attempting to do (*side note, I brought my Slam acceptance letter with me; something told me to and I'm glad I listened*). She looks at me for a moment and says, "ok". She also says she will have my Godfather drive me and one of my God-brothers come with me. *Support of your loved ones makes your confidence super high.*

The next day comes and I'm up early to wash and eat breakfast. While the rest of the family goes to the Disney parks, my Godfather and God brother will take me over to Disney's Wide World of Sports Institute. *Now remember there is no guarantee but, I'm going to make the effort.*

When we arrive to the complex, we get to the security post and the guard asks why we are there? I'm sitting in the front seat and I tell the guard I work for Slam Magazine and I'm here to cover the USA Basketball Team and then I show her my letter.

She takes the letter, calls somebody and then tells them my name and who I am representing. A few minutes go by and she tells me what building I must go to, which was Studio 9 and 10 to apply for my credentials.

She gives us a parking pass and then we ride over to Studio 9 and 10. When we park, we are instructed to enter Studio 9. I enter Studio 9, and this is the media center for USA Basketball. There are two older ladies who are extremely polite, and they ask for my name and the letter I showed the security guard, and they take it and make a copy. *I'm now thinking to myself is this really going to happen???* The lady comes back and asks can she speak to someone from the office. I tell her yes and she asks for the phone number and contact person. She then tells me to take a seat and she will get back to me.

About 15-20 minutes go by and she comes back out and calls me up and lets me know I'm approved. *Are you kidding me? This is crazy!* She then asks me for the correct spelling of my name and then makes a label that she places on my USA Basketball credential. She then gives me my media packet and instructs me to building 10. She also gives me two additional credentials for My Godfather and God brother. *God is truly blessing me, this is unbelievable.*

We enter Building 10 and this is the practice gym for USA Basketball, and I show my media credentials and I'm directed towards the court and there is a designated section for the media. I am witnessing the USA Basketball team scrimmaging. *I know you are probably thinking, why are they in Orlando? Well, this was their training camp location before departing for Atlanta.*

The media director comes out and says the court will be open in 10 minutes and players and coaches will then be available for questions. My God father and

God Brother by this time had found the catering station.

The court then opens up and I have my camera, pad and pen. *Today I'm a reporter lol.* When I get on the court, the players are paired off shooting free throws and I proceed to take pics. But, before I know it, the players are coming to the sidelines and reporters are in front of them asking questions. *Lol, I don't know what to do.*

Then I see Lenny Wilkens, head coach of the team and I introduce myself. He tells me I have a bright future. I then see Mitch Richmond and ask him a few questions about the Kings upcoming season. The main stars are swarmed. The media director then says the session is over and he will see us tomorrow at 10am. (*What, another day of this? This is the life.*) As I'm leaving, Shaq walks out and I spot him. *Now it's forbidden for credentialed media to ask for an autograph but, whatever!!!*

So, I ask for his autograph and his pic and he obliges and takes a pic with me and my God brother. I tell him why I am there he then says, "that's good lil bro keep working hard".

We leave from there and go back to the house we are staying, when the family get back, I tell them everything. My God Mom and Mom smiles at me and says "good work".

The next day I'm up early and I'm ready. That morning I read that newspaper and the big story is about the reality of Shaq leaving the Magics for the Lakers. I'm determined this time around to comfortably and ask Shaq, is he leaving? So, when we get there, the women are practicing i.e., Lisa Leslie, Dawn Staley, Cheryl Cooper. Their practice ends and then the men's practice starts, and this is basketball. Like I never saw everything this sharp and a missed shot is rare. There is a lot shit talking go on with Gary Payton, Charles Barkley and Reggie Miller leading it.

Then practice ends and this time I have a plan. I'm going to get to Penny Hardaway and anybody player after that is icing on the cake. So, when practice ends, I spot the basket Penny is shooting on and I make my way towards it. I do this because once he is done, this is probably where he will be speaking to the reporters.

Sure enough, the media session is open, and he sits right under the basket and I'm the first over there. I introduce myself and ask for a picture he says yes and I ask him about the upcoming Olympic games. Now I move around and get a chance to speak to Hakeem Olajuwon, Reggie Miller, Charles Barkley, Gary Payton and then boom guess who was walking by? Shaq, and this is my "can't get knocked down moment".

I looked up to him and reintroduce myself and then ask him if I can something, he says sure lil bro. I say to him "You should stay with The Magic, you and Penny can be the modern day, Magic and Kareem. You can win a lot of championships together. Are you going to stay?" He looks down at me and laughs then shakes his head and says, "Thanks lil bro" and he gives me the same stare you give somebody that offers you advice about a situation, but you already decided on which decision you going to make.

The media session is over, and this is the last day of practice before they leave for Atlanta. *That experience gave me even more motivation to continue to work towards having a position in the business of basketball.* I'm so excited when I get back to the vacation house! The next morning, I wake up to get the newspaper. It's July 18, 1996 and guess what the headline is "Bye Bye Mickey, Hello Hollywood, Shaq Signs with The Lakers".

Guess he didn't listen to me lol and welcome to the harsh reality of the business of basketball.

Chapter 18: Faith.

The summer of 96 is almost over and already, I've covered the USA Basketball team, met Maurice Cheeks who gave me an insight on Allen Iverson. At that point, my entrepreneur spirit kicks in. I decide I'm going to make my own publication called 'The Full Court Press'.

This will be a basketball informative tool with an emphasis on stats and game analysis with a hip-hop flavor, basically Slam's nephew. I decide to do a 97-97 NBA preview and the pics that I use, would be from me covering the USA Basketball practices in Orlando.

I put together this detailed NBA preview for all 30 teams and arranged the photos to coincide with the details of the preview. When it's complete, I said to myself, "I'm going to bring this to service and present it to the Loa so it can be blessed, and then I will make my mark on the basketball world".

Sunday service is rolling, the drums are rocking you can feel the power of God within service and then we start the singing the songs/prayers for Papa Ogu, the Loa of truth, strength, and faith. When my Godmother possesses the power of Papa Ogu, he begins to service the people by speaking to them and giving them messages of advice to uplift them in their life.

I go to one of the male priests and explain to him that I need to speak to the Loa about a project I'm working. I explain my project to him, and he agrees and takes me to the Loa.

When I approach the Loa Papa Ogu, I explain to him that I would like help with my magazine to be successful. The Loa leaned back and took a puff of his cigar and says, it's good what I did but I need to create a basketball league because it will have a bigger impact then a magazine. The priest then explains to me that magazine success is based on advertisement, not issue sale and that I need to listen to the guidance the Loa has given me. I tell the Loa yes and thank you, but as I leave to go back to dancing and singing in the service I'm thinking, "how am I going to create a basketball league?" *Six years later, I would have the answer.*

It's now the fall of '96 and I return to Drexel as a night student. I'm taking corporate relations and marketing classes at night and due to my experience working in the bookstore at CCP I'm able to gain employment at the Drexel Bookstore. My routine is work in the morning till mid-afternoon and then play in the gym and class in the evening.

During my time playing in the gym, I became friendly with members of the basketball team primarily because I was one of the few black males from the inner city on campus just like the members of the basketball team. In particular, I became extremely tight with the returning senior who was from South Philly along with the two incoming freshmen, one from Chester and the other from Philly, who happened to play for my Sonny Hill team after I moved on.

The returning senior from South Philly was a returning starter and all conference player who was a key component in Drexel defeating Memphis, the season before in the NCAA Tournament. We became cool due to our similar background along with knowing some of the same people. Life is stable and progressing in an upright direction. The 1996-97 season starts, and I have access to all of the Drexel games and my high school teammate is now a senior starter at the Top 10, nationally ranked, Villanova, along with being an NBA draft prospect.

I have an up-close view of two of the Philadelphia Division One college basketball programs which both are having success and to top it off my Slam Promo position is providing me access to a lot of the high-level high school basketball games. With the access that I have gained, I'm becoming known in the Philly basketball community as the "Slam Guy".

There was a complete difference between the two school's season expectations. Villanova had Final 4 expectations due to them having three returning starters and a McDonalds All American who would be a one and done along with several national televised games. Drexel on the other hand was in a mid-major conference coming off "One Shining Moment" during March Madness and had only one starter returning along with three players who weren't rotation players along with no nationally televised games and the only way for them to make the tournament is by winning their conference tourney.

The season for the respective teams didn't live up to their expectations. Drexel had an up and down season due to the fact they had a senior leading a bunch of young guys who were getting acclimated to college basketball their season ended by losing to its archrival in the conference tourney. Villanova's season was a disappointment considering all the preseason hype they had and to make it worse, they lost in the second round of the NCAA Tournament to a team outside of the Top 25 whose star player would go to be an NFL Hall of Famer. (*Go figure.*)

It was interesting to see the differences between a major college basketball program and a mid-major program whereas Drexel facilities and amenities were one you expect from a high-level prep school team. Villanova's program had unlimited inventory of apparel, they traveled chartered, they had a practice facility, and they played their home games at the core state center and sold out the arena.

Every week, I would attend at least two games rather it was a high school or college game. And just like when I attended Sonny Hill and 16th street games, I would study the organization of the game atmosphere, along with the apparel of the teams. Honestly, I became a business of basketball junkie and what really put it in overdrive was a letter I received in December 1996.

Chapter 19: Results.

Remember earlier I was telling you about my David Falk letter writing campaign? Well mind you, this is super-agent David Falk, agent for the global icon, Michael Jordan and Allen Iverson, and the leader of the hip hop culture being integrated in basketball. I started writing letters monthly in February to David Falk, along with calling and trying to arrange a meeting with him. In the process, his assistant Mary Ellen became very familiar with my name. That was due to me being persistent and borderline annoying/stalkerish.

On December 8, 1996, I come home from school and I check the mail and it's a letter from FAME aka Falk Associates Management Enterprises. So, I rush into the house and open the letter and I be damn it's a letter from David Falk himself on his letterhead and it reads:

"Dear Rahim,

Thank you for your most recent letter dated December 3, 1996. I have truly been impressed with your persistence and desire in working for me and F.A.M.E, however as Mary Ellen indicated in her conversation last week with you, we are, at this time, fully staffed and have no plans to hire any new personnel and/or interns in the near future. Again, thank you for your interest and I wish you much continued success at Drexel University this coming January and in your future endeavors. I have no doubt that your ambition, enthusiasm, and motivation will take you far.

Sincerely,
David Falk"

That letter provided me with unlimited courage to keep working hard. Super-agent David Falk took time out of his busy schedule to write me a detailed inspiring letter to a young black man living in North Philly who has aspirations of success in the business of basketball. *God is the all-knowing and as long as you are work hard and don't cut corners and are honest, consistent, and forthright, he will bless you with fuel to keep your fire and passion always burning.*

Now a few weeks later, another blessing came my way as the late great John Wooden said, "luck is when preparation meets opportunity" so it's now the 1996-97 NBA season and Allen Iverson is on fire. He has taken the NBA global world by storm and here in Philadelphia, even though the 76ers aren't having a winning season, he has brought excitement and hope to the city in regard to professional basketball. Meanwhile, the Chicago Bulls are the defending champs and are seeking their fifth NBA Championship in the past seven years.

They are scheduled to play the 76ers on Saturday December 21st in their first of two appearances in

Philadelphia and this will be the first time MJ plays AI in front of Philadelphia fans. I have to be there this time. I have to witness this matchup with my own two eyes. So, I contact one of the ticket scalpers I know from my Temple basketball days. Now remember, I'm working and going to school so I do have the ability to sacrifice and purchase a ticket.

When I get in contact with him, I let him know I need one ticket for the game, and he tells me it's the upper level and the price will be $150. (*Damn that's kind of steep and these are the days before stub hub, etc.*). He assures me it's a good seat with a solid view (*smh*), so I arrange to meet him before the game to make the transaction.

It's game day and the game starts at 7:30pm and we are supposed to meet at 6pm. Now FYI, the $150 is half of my weekly check from the bookstore so this is a major purchase for me. I take the Broad Street Line subway to Pattison Avenue. When I exit the train, I walk up the stairs and exit the subway and who do I see, my former ticket scalper from Temple. When I see him, I ask him what tickets he has available and he just laughs at me and says he has all uppers, and they are starting at $250 which is $100 more then I'm spending so I tell him I'm good and I go on to meet up with the other scalper.

So, when we meet up, he shows me the seating chart and the seats are in the upper level 200 section, same as my guy from Temple but they are $100 cheaper, and it will get me into the game, but these can be considered nosebleed seats and I would have a better view on TV, but the game is on cable and I don't have cable (*go figure*). So, I give him the money and he gives me the ticket.

I should be happy but I'm not and the reason why is because this was not the seat, I expected for this soon to be historical event. I'm appreciative for the entrance but this isn't what I wanted and needed. Then I hear in my head be patient just relax and don't enter the arena yet. So, I step away from the guy who I brought the ticket from and I go to the sidewalk leading to the arena and wait.

As I'm waiting there counting down the time for tip off, an older white man with a resemblance towards Santa Clause, I mean glasses, white beard and weight asks me would I like to attend the game. I look at him weirdly and I reply, "Yes I would, I have a ticket, but it isn't for a very good seat." He then replies, "I have a single ticket and you can have it, Merry Christmas from the 76ers House band". He gives me the ticket and its completely opposite of the one I have; it has Allen Iverson picture on it and it's in the lower-level Section 106 Row 9 Seat 7. By time I look back up, the man is gone.

I'm completely shocked, did this really happen? Did I just see Saint Nicholas? Is this a Christmas Miracle? Just a little piece of advice to the reader, when you hear that voice in your head tell you something, you should definitely listen because it's the Loa or the Holy Spirit guiding and protecting you.

So now I can enter the arena and as I'm getting in line to enter the arena, I see a young black kid selling candy I stop and ask him how much are they? He responds, "they are a dollar". I then say," how about I trade you a ticket to the game in exchange for a candy bar?", He looks at me like I'm crazy and then I show him the upper-level ticket he says are you serious and I said yea and I give him the ticket and he walks away, and I tell him to keep the candy bar.

Now when I get to the door the ticket attendant takes my ticket and rips the admission part of my ticket, (*mind you this is before the technology of scanning tickets*) and tells me happy holidays and enjoy the game. I'm so excited. I'm in the arena at a game that millions of fans across the world want to be at and here I am, blessed to be in the building.

As I enter my section I stopped and ask the usher where is the 76ers House Band? The usher looks at me with an odd look and says there is no such thing as the 76ers House Band. So, I go to my seat and I think to myself "was that really Saint Nicholas aka Santa Clause that I met?" *This is a question I ask every time around Christmas.*

Let me tell you something. This game was amazing. The Bulls showed why they are the champions and why Michael Jordan is the icon he is. But Allen Iverson makes it clear that he will be a game changer and a force to be reckoned with for years to come. There is one thing about this game a lot of people don't know. When MJ went to guard AI on the switch from Ron Harper, the refs called illegal defense and bailed him out. It's the second time that they played the Bulls at home and in the switch, you hear Phil

Jackson yell "Michael" and Iverson did the legendary crossover of Jordan. *The month of December 1996 would set me on my business path of basketball for the next 20 years.*

Choose Wisely!

Photos

1992-93 Olney Varsity

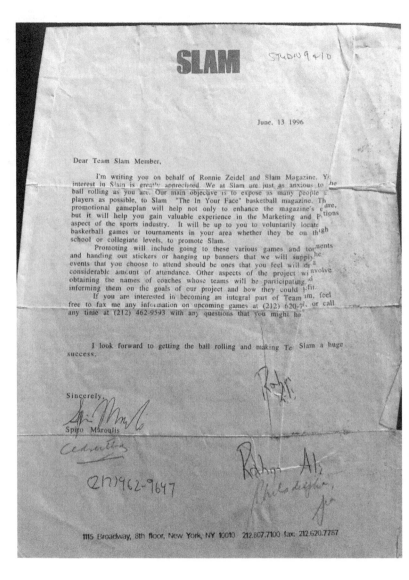

SLAM

STUDIO 410

June, 13 1996

Dear Team Slam Member,

I'm writing you on behalf of Ronnie Zeidel and Slam Magazine. Your interest in Slam is greatly appreciated. We at Slam are just as anxious to the ball rolling as you are. Our main objective is to expose as many people as players as possible, to Slam "The In Your Face" basketball magazine. The promotional gameplan will help not only to enhance the magazine's culture, but it will help you gain valuable experience in the Marketing and Promotions aspect of the sports industry. It will be up to you to voluntarily locate basketball games or tournaments in your area whether they be on th high school or collegiate levels, to promote Slam.

Promoting will include going to these various games and torments and handing out stickers or hanging up banners that we will supply the events that you choose to attend should be ones that you feel will draw a considerable amount of attendance. Other aspects of the project will involve obtaining the names of coaches whose teams will be participating and informing them on the goals of our project and how they could benefit.

If you are interested in becoming an integral part of Team Slam, feel free to fax me any information on upcoming games at (212) 620-7, or call any time at (212) 462-9593 with any questions that you might have

I look forward to getting the ball rolling and making Team Slam a huge success.

Sincerely,

Spiro Maroulis

(212) 962-9647

1115 Broadway, 8th floor, New York, NY 10010   212.807.7100 fax: 212.620.7787

-1996 SLAM Acceptance Letter

100

-1996 USA Basketball Media Credential.

-1996 The Day Before Shaq Signed with The Lakers

-1996 Penny Hardaway

The Full Court Press

$2.00

-1996 The Full Court Press

F.A.M.E.
FALK ASSOCIATES MANAGEMENT ENTERPRISES

DAVID B. FALK
Chairman/CEO

December 4, 1996

Mr. Rahim K. Ali
1527 B North 16th Street
Philadelphia, PA 19121

Dear Rahim:

Thank you for your most recent letter dated December 3, 1996. I have truly been impressed with your persistence and desire in working for me and F.A.M.E. However, as Mary Ellen indicated in her conversation last week with you, we are, at this time, fully staffed and have no plans to hire any new personnel and/or interns in the near future.

Again, thank you for your interest and I wish you much continued success at Drexel University this coming January and in your future endeavors. I have no doubt that your ambition, enthusiasm and motivation will take your far.

Sincerely,

David B. Falk

DBF:men

6135 WISCONSIN AVENUE, NW • SUITE 850 • WASHINGTON, DC 20015 • TELEPHONE: (202) 686-2000 • FACSIMILE: (202) 686-5050

-1996 Letter from David Falk

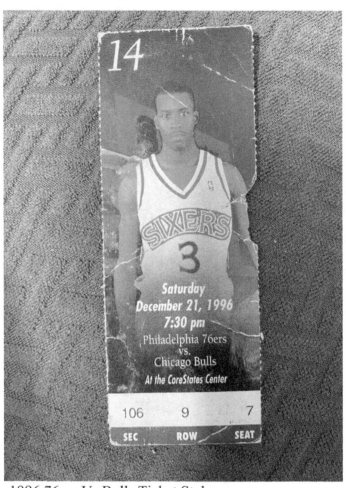

-1996 76ers Vs Bulls Ticket Stub

Rahim Thompson, a 44-year-old black male, married to his wife, Tanisha Thompson of 9 years and counting. They share two beautiful daughters, 9 years old, Veriteady and 7 years old, Klerekado. They all live together along with Rahim's mother ,72-year-old Octavia Danielson who is a retired law clerk.

Rahim is A Gro Houngan (male high Voodoo priest), of 9 Years at Le Peristyle Haitian Sanctuary, who's purpose is to show the beauty & truth of the Voodoo religion and dispel the myths and biases of the Voodoo faith. Rahim Thompson is also the founder and owner of The Chosen League, a nationally recognized high school basketball leagued based out of Philadelphia, Pennsylvania, sponsored by organizations including Nike, the Philadelphia 76ers, Mitchell & Ness, & Baby Blues Bbq.

Made in the USA
Monee, IL
22 March 2021

62683087R00066